potato favourites

PENGUIN BOOKS

Food in a
minute®

potato
favourites

allyson gofton

PENGUIN BOOKS

PENGUIN BOOKS

Published by the Penguin Group

Penguin Group (NZ), 67 Apollo Drive, Rosedale,

North Shore 0632, New Zealand (a division of Pearson New Zealand Ltd)

Penguin Group (USA) Inc., 375 Hudson Street,

New York, New York 10014, USA

Penguin Group (Canada), 90 Eglinton Avenue East, Suite 700, Toronto,

Ontario, M4P 2Y3, Canada (a division of Pearson Penguin Canada Inc.)

Penguin Books Ltd, 80 Strand, London, WC2R 0RL, England

Penguin Ireland, 25 St Stephen's Green,

Dublin 2, Ireland (a division of Penguin Books Ltd)

Penguin Group (Australia), 250 Camberwell Road, Camberwell,

Victoria 3124, Australia (a division of Pearson Australia Group Pty Ltd)

Penguin Books India Pvt Ltd, 11, Community Centre,

Panchsheel Park, New Delhi – 110 017, India

Penguin Books (South Africa) (Pty) Ltd, 24 Sturdee Avenue,

Rosebank, Johannesburg 2196, South Africa

Penguin Books Ltd, Registered Offices: 80 Strand, London, WC2R 0RL, England

First published by Penguin Group (NZ), 2008

1 3 5 7 9 10 8 6 4 2

Designed by Seven

Prepress by Image Centre Ltd

Printed in China through Bookbuilders, Hong Kong

Commissioning Editor Alison Brook

Managing Editor Andrea Coppock

ISBN: 978 0 14 300921 4

A catalogue record for this book is available
from the National Library of New Zealand.

www.penguin.co.nz

One potato, two potato,
Three potato, four,
Five potato, six potato,
Seven potato, more!

introduction

Spuds, tatties, taters . . . whatever you call them, potatoes have long been a staple of life around the world. The Incas were eating (and worshipping) them in fifth century BC South America, from where sixteenth-century explorers brought them to Europe. Seed potatoes came to New Zealand with the early settlers and the crops sustained pioneer families, for whom they were often a substitute for meat. Potatoes continue to be one of the most popular vegetables for the home garden and our number 1 purchased vegetable.

Boil, bake, roast or fry; serve hot or cold, in or out of their jackets, creamed or plain, potatoes can be eaten at any meal. Potatoes can make a dish on their own, be an integral part of a meal or an accompaniment to a wide range of other foods for everyday tables and special occasions.

With a number of varieties to choose from year round, each with its own qualities to enable the cook to obtain the perfect result, all you need are recipes and, in this book, I have collated an eclectic collection. Some are old favourites, some take a new look at one of our favourite vegetables and all of them are very easy to prepare. Ignore the anti-potato/starch brigade – in moderation, potatoes are nothing but good for you.

'Potatoes served at breakfast;
At dinner served again;
Potatoes served at supper,
Forever and Amen!'
(An old Pennsylvanian prayer)

ENJOY!

allyson gofton

potato know how

which spud to use

Choose potatoes that do not have any cuts, bruises, green patches or shoots. Sometimes you may choose a smooth-looking potato over a misshapen one and assume that it is a better product. This is not necessarily the case as some varieties characteristically have skins which are netted or have eyes in them. A potato does not have to look good to cook brilliantly! Different potatoes will cook differently – so you need to use a potato suited to your *end use*.

Buying potatoes by end use means buying potatoes that will give the best result for that particular recipe. These potatoes will have been cook-tested by the growers or packers and will cook according to the packaging. They will be marked as for 'boiling', 'salads', 'wedges' or 'baking'. For best results select the right potato for the job.

At either end of the spectrum, a potato is either 'floury' or 'waxy'. Some potatoes are less floury or less waxy than others. These potatoes fall in the area of 'general-purpose' and will tend to perform most tasks, although perhaps with not as good results as the ones that clearly fall into the floury or waxy category.

Waxy
Ideal for boiling, salads, casseroles, soups.
Most early (new) season potatoes
Nadine
Draga
Frisia

Limited or localised supply: Jersey Bennie, Liseta, Red King Edward, Tiffany

General-purpose
Suitable for most end uses.
Rua
Desirée
Karaka
Moonlight

Limited or localised supply: Red Ruby, Rocket, Maris Anchor

Floury
Ideal for mashing, wedges, roasting, chips, baking.
Ilam Hardy
Red Rascal
Agria (and the related varieties Bolesta and Markie)
Fianna

Limited or localised supply: White Delight, Victoria

how to store spuds

Store them in a well-ventilated, cool, dark place. Don't put them in the fridge as the flavour changes will be noticeable. Always remove them from any plastic packaging, unless it is a 'Greenguard' bag, which are manufactured specifically for potatoes. Place them gently in your storage area because even though they look tough they do bruise easily. A heavy paper bag or cardboard box makes a good storage container.

Waxy

Nadine	Draga	Frisia	Cooked

General-purpose

Rua	Desirée	Karaka	Moonlight	Cooked

Floury

Ilam Hardy	Red Rascal	Agria	Fianna	Cooked

spuds are good for you

Natural dirt and dust on potatoes can help to keep them fresher so it is best not to wash them until you are ready to cook them – or if you buy ready washed, buy small quantities regularly.

The potato has been described as the phytochemical jewel box. They are a great fuel food to power your body and provide a wealth of nutrients, especially vitamin C and potassium. As we eat so many potatoes, New Zealanders get around 30% of their vitamin C requirement from them. They are a valuable source of B group vitamins, particularly B6, thiamin and niacin. Potatoes are also a good source of fibre and they contain some iron and magnesium. They are high in starch so will stop you feeling hungry for a long time. Antioxidants present in potatoes are phenolic acids, vitamin C, and in yellow-fleshed or red-skinned varieties – carotenoids and anthocyanins respectively. Potatoes are also a source of high-quality protein.

Potatoes are not fattening; however, some cooking and preparation methods are!

kumara know how

which kumara to buy and use

Roast kumara is about as Kiwi as it gets and there are three main varieties commercially grown and available.

1. The most common is the Owairaka Red, with its classic red skin and dusty yellow flesh. It remains quite firm when cooked and is ideal to roast or boil and to make kumara fishcakes or similar.

2. Toka Toka Gold has desert-yellow skin and golden-yellow flesh and is very sweet. It has a medium–firm texture when cooked and is really an all-purpose kumara in cooking terms.

3. The orange kumara with its red/brown-coloured skin and deep orange flesh is the sweetest and softest of all the kumara and is best used where you will have a moist cooking method, like mashing, or in curries and making into soup. Orange kumara is sometimes sold as Beauregard.

how to buy and store kumara

Look for kumara that are firm to the touch and have an unbroken skin. Kumara are best bought weekly, never refrigerate as they will shrivel and could begin to decay.

kumara are good for you

Kumara are a valuable source of vitamin C, iron, potassium and calcium. The coloured skin and flesh of kumara carries an array of phytochemicals. Varieties with red or purple skins or flesh contain anthocyanins, and those with orange and yellow pigments are rich in alpha-carotene. The richer the colour, the more anthocyanins and alpha-carotene. Kumara can be prepared in exactly the same way as potatoes. It's not always necessary to peel them. If possible, scrub thoroughly and leave the skin on for best nutritional value.

Potatoes and kumara used in this book were purchased at local supermarkets and greengrocers. Potatoes required in the recipes are listed as waxy, starchy, baking, etc. Choose a variety that is available at the time of purchase. Where kumara are used, use the variety of your choice when a specific variety is not specified.

spices and herbs to go with potatoes

spices

ajowan	curry leaves	mustard
allspice	dill	nigella
amchoor	fennel	nutmeg
anise	fenugreek	paprika
annatto	galangal	pepper
capers	ginger	poppy
caraway	juniper	saffron
cardamom	kaffir lime	sesame
cinnamon	kokam	star anise
cloves	lemon grass	sumac
coriander	lemon myrtle	tamarind
cumin	mace	turmeric

herbs

basil	garlic chives	salad burnet
bay	horseradish	sorrel
borage	lovage	summer and
celery	marjoram	winter savoury
chervil	mint	tarragon
chives	oregano	thyme
coriander	rocket	watercress
dill	rosemary	
fennel	sage	

potato culinary kitchen

The humble spud has probably spawned more culinary utensils than any other single food. From peeler to masher, slicer to ricer, it's available to make the job at hand that much easier or look that much more professional. All these items are available at good cook shops.

Potato Mit With all those wonderful nutrients just under the skin of the potato, try to eat them unpeeled when you can. While they mostly come well-washed and ready to cook, some varieties from the local market still require washing and the excess dirt to be scrubbed off. Put your hands into these coarse-textured potato mits and make the job easy. Hang over the taps to dry.

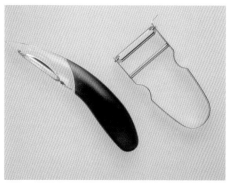

Peeler Coming in all shapes and sizes, the humble peeler would have to be one of the simplest but most useful kitchen tools ever. With all the variations, they come with blades of varying quality. For left-handed people make sure you buy one with a reversible blade and not a set blade. And if you love spuds in your home, the point at the end of the blade is designed to pick out any blemishes. Dry well before putting away to avoid rusting. And as these implements are not too expensive, replace them when bluntish – you will notice the difference.

Wavy Cutter Coming in many guises the wavy cutter can make crinkle-cut chips with ease. For safe use, cut a thin base from the potato so that it sits without rocking on the chopping board and press the wavy cutter down through the spud. Toss in oil, season with salt and bake in a hot oven until golden.

Potato Ricer For the softest, fluffiest mashed potatoes (just like chefs prepare), a ricer will do the trick. Great for dryish starches, like potatoes or red-skinned kumara, as the cooked vegetable is pressed through a fine mesh. The metal bucket base is filled

with cooked potato and then the pusher bears down, pressing the potato through the mesh base. In some models the base can be removed and replaced by one with smaller or larger holes to achieve your preferred smooth mash. After that, add a hearty knob of butter and a good dash of milk plus seasonings and the fluffiest mashed spuds are yours to enjoy.

Masher Oh, the unassuming masher. I like the classic traditional wavy masher. They're easy to use, will mash the potatoes in the pot they were cooked in, are inexpensive, last a lifetime and are efficient. In a word – essential. While your spud purée will not be as smooth as that prepared in a ricer, it will still be fabulous.

Potato Chip Cutter It takes such a short amount of time to make your own chips that a manual potato chipper is a handy item to include in the cupboard. A basic model is all that is required. Prepare the potato or kumara and simply place in the centre cavity of the unit and press firmly on the handle to force the potato through the nastily sharp grid. Simple and surprisingly little effort or force is required. And don't forget to soak the chips for 30 minutes in water before deep frying. Dry well before plunging into hot fat. For a healthier version, scatter the freshly chipped spuds on a tray and toss in a little oil and bake at a high temperature until crispy and golden.

Mandolin For thinly sliced potatoes or kumara, a mandolin makes light work of the task. They are available in very simple styles, such as the version shown here, or the more elaborate and robust professional versions that rest on a board and come with adjustable blades for slicing, shredding, julienne, pomme gaufrettes (lattice-style slices) and chips. Price and need will determine your choice.

thai potato wedges with
thai peanut dip   16

lemon and pepper
potato wedges   18

wedges and dips   21
· avocado and blue
  cheese dip
· mexican tomato and
  olive dip

other dips   23
· apricot, onion and cream
  cheese dip
· olive and tomato dip
· creamy dill and caper dip

kumara chips   24
· moroccan tomato dip
· sour cream, mustard and
  honey dip

new potato canapés   27

nibbles

1 kilogram starchy potatoes,
    scrubbed
1 egg
2 tablespoons water
3 tablespoons flour
1 tablespoon Thai red
    curry paste
oil for shallow frying

thai peanut dip

1 medium onion, peeled
    and finely diced
2 teaspoons minced garlic
1 teaspoon minced ginger
2 stalks lemon grass,
    trimmed and finely
    chopped (optional)

1 tablespoon Thai
    curry paste
1 cup coconut milk
½ cup Eta Smooth or
    Crunchy Peanut Butter

thai potato wedges with thai peanut dip

serves 12
preparation time **20 minutes** cooking time **30 minutes**

Cut the potatoes into long chunky
wedges. Blanch in boiling salted water
for 10 minutes or until almost cooked.
Drain well and dry on an absorbent
paper towel.

Beat together the egg, water, flour,
curry paste and a good seasoning
of salt.

Heat enough oil to cover the base of a
wide deep-sided frying-pan to about
0.5-cm depth and heat.

Toss the potatoes in the egg mixture
allowing any excess to fall off. Place
6–8 wedges into the hot oil and turn
over a moderately hot heat until
lightly brown and tender. Keep warm.

Serve hot with the thai peanut dip.

thai peanut dip
Heat a dash of oil in a frying-pan and
cook the onion over a low heat for 5–8
minutes until tender. Add the garlic,
ginger, lemon grass and Thai curry
paste and cook a further 2 minutes. Add
the coconut milk and the peanut butter
and stir only until warm. Do not boil.

600–700 grams starchy or
  all-purpose potatoes

2 tablespoons lemon and
  pepper seasoning

½ lemon, juice

¼ cup olive oil

1 tablespoon finely chopped
  fresh rosemary

lemon and pepper dip

250-gram pottle sour cream

2–3 teaspoons lemon and
  pepper seasoning

1 teaspoon prepared mild
  mustard

lemon and pepper potato wedges

serves 8

preparation time **15 minutes** cooking time **25 minutes**

Wash the potatoes well and cut into large chunky wedges and place in a large bowl. Toss with the lemon and pepper seasoning, lemon juice, olive oil and rosemary. Scatter in one layer on a baking paper-lined tray.

Bake at 200 °C for 20–25 minutes or until the chips are golden and tender. Serve quickly once cooked with the lemon and pepper dip.

lemon and pepper dip

For the dip stir all the ingredients together.

allyson's tips

· Vary the dip by adding a handful of chopped parsley or chives or a teaspoon of finely chopped green peppercorns.

· For a thinner sauce, thin with a little cream, milk or water.

did you know

The original meaning of the word spud does not refer to the potato itself, but to the implement used to dig the potato out of the ground in the years before the invention of the plough.

allyson's tip

Avocado and blue cheese
dip: For a creamier dip mix
in ½–1 cup sour cream.

1-kilogram bag Wattie's
Frozen Golden Heart
Jacket Wedges

**avocado and blue
cheese dip**

170-gram pottle Wattie's
Frozen Chunky Avocado,
defrosted

50 grams blue cheese,
crumbled

2 spring onions, trimmed
and very finely chopped

1 red chilli, deseeded and
finely chopped

**mexican tomato and
olive dip**

400-gram can Wattie's
Mexican Style Tomatoes

1 lime, grated rind

¼ cup pitted black olives,
finely chopped

2 spring onions, trimmed
and finely chopped

2–3 tablespoons chopped
fresh coriander

wedges and dips

serves 10
preparation time **2 minutes** cooking time **30 minutes**

Arrange the wedges in a single layer
on a baking paper-lined oven tray.

Bake at 230 °C for 25–30 minutes,
turning if wished, until crispy
and golden.

Serve immediately with one of the
following dips.

**avocado and blue cheese dip
makes 1 cup**
preparation time **10 minutes**
Place all the ingredients in a small
bowl and mix well to combine or place
in a food processor and process until
smooth. Serve with hot wedges.

**mexican tomato and olive dip
serves 10**
preparation time **10 minutes**
Place the tomatoes in a food processor
and process until smooth.

Pour into a small bowl and stir in the
lime rind, olives, spring onion and
coriander and serve with hot wedges.

For other dips (see page 23):
· apricot, onion and cream cheese dip
· olive and tomato dip
· creamy dill and caper dip

allyson's tips

- Apricot, onion and cream cheese dip: Add a few finely chopped dried apricots if wished. A little grated orange rind is delicious here as well.

- Creamy dill and caper dip: If you do not have dill, other herbs that work well here include parsley, chives and fennel. If you like a tartare sauce, add 1 tablespoon of finely chopped gherkins.

did you know

Around 55% of the local potato crop is targeted for processing.

22

apricot, onion and cream cheese dip

½ cup Wattie's Bit on the Side Spiced Apricot Sauce

2–3 spring onions, finely chopped

2 tablespoons finely chopped fresh chives

½ cup cream cheese

olive and tomato dip

¾ cup Wattie's Classic Mayonnaise or sour cream

50 grams feta cheese, crumbled

¼ cup stuffed green olives, finely chopped

4 semi-dried tomatoes, finely chopped

1–2 tablespoons chopped fresh basil

1 teaspoon garlic, optional

creamy dill and caper dip

1 cup Wattie's Classic Mayonnaise or sour cream or cream cheese

1 lime, grated rind and juice

2 tablespoons chopped fresh dill or 1 tablespoon dried dill

2 tablespoons capers, chopped

other dips
to go with wedges

apricot, onion and cream cheese dip
serves 10

preparation time **10 minutes**
Place all the ingredients in a small bowl and mix well to combine or place in a food processor and process until smooth. Serve with hot wedges.

olive and tomato dip
serves 10

preparation time **10 minutes**
Place all the ingredients in a small bowl and mix well until smooth or place in a food processor and process until smooth. Thin with milk if wished.

Serve as a dip with wedges or roasters.

creamy dill and caper dip
serves 10

preparation time **10 minutes**
Place all the ingredients in a small bowl and mix well or place in a food processor and process until smooth. Serve with hot wedges.

1-kilogram bag Wattie's
Frozen Golden Heart
Kumara Chips

moroccan tomato dip
400-gram can Wattie's
Moroccan Style Tomatoes
1 orange, grated rind
1 teaspoon brown sugar

**sour cream, mustard
and honey dip**
250-gram pottle sour cream
or lite sour cream
2 tablespoons prepared mild
mustard
1 tablespoon honey

kumara chips

serves 8
preparation time **5 minutes** cooking time **20 minutes**

Scatter the frozen kumara chips onto
a baking paper-lined tray.

Bake at 230 °C for 20 minutes or until
hot and golden.

Serve with one of the following dips.

moroccan tomato dip
makes 1¼ cups
preparation time **10 minutes**
Put all the ingredients in a food
processor and process until smooth.

sour cream, mustard and honey dip
makes 1 cup
preparation time **5 minutes**
Stir all the ingredients together.

allyson's tip

For this recipe you need
even-sized roundish
potatoes. I used Nadines
in our photo.

500 grams baby new
    potatoes (approximately
    16), scrubbed

tuna and mayo topping
½ cup Wattie's Classic
    Mayonnaise
½ cup cream cheese
85-gram pouch Greenseas
    Tuna Chunks in
    Springwater
Around 16 capers, halved
Sprigs of small basil leaves
    or torn large leaves

avocado and olive topping
170-gram pottle Wattie's
    Frozen Chunky Avocado,
    defrosted
8 cherry tomatoes,
    quartered
8–12 olives, sliced
Small sprigs coriander or
    parsley leaves

new potato canapés

makes 32
preparation time **15 minutes** cooking time **15 minutes**

Cook the potatoes in a pot of salted
water over a gentle simmer for 15
minutes or until just tender.

Drain, refresh in cold water, drain and
leave covered to cool.

Use a serrated paring knife to halve
each potato and arrange on a platter.

Top with either the tuna and mayo or
avocado and olive topping.

tuna and mayo topping
Mix the mayonnaise and cream
cheese together. Top each potato half
with a little of the mixture. Divide the
tuna among the potatoes and garnish
with the capers and basil leaves.

avocado and olive topping
Top the potatoes with even amounts
of avocado and decorate with the
tomatoes, olives and coriander or
parsley leaves.

soups

2 onions, peeled and finely
   diced
4–6 rashers bacon, diced
750 grams waxy potatoes,
   peeled and diced
2 stalks celery, trimmed and
   finely chopped
5 cups light beef stock
1–2 cups Wattie's Frozen
   Broad Beans, blanched
   and peeled
½ cup chopped fresh parsley

bacon and potato soup

serves 4
preparation time **15 minutes** cooking time **30 minutes**

Cook the onion and bacon in a large
saucepan until very fragrant and the
onions are well softened (about 15
minutes).

Add the potato and celery and cook
for a further 2–3 minutes, tossing or
stirring regularly.

Add the beef stock and simmer gently
for 10–12 minutes until the potato is
tender.

Add the broad beans during the last
1–2 minutes of cooking time.

Add the parsley and serve immediately
with crusty bread rolls.

did you know

- One potato, two potato, three potato, four, five potato, six potato, seven potato, more . . . is a playground game, enjoyed the world over by children.

They stand in a circle and hold out their hands in a fist with thumbs up. The leader takes one fist and begins counting off each fist by gently tapping them. When the leader needs to count his/her counting fist, he/she taps it on the chin. When the leader gets to 'more', the child tapped puts that fist behind his/her back. The rhyme is repeated until only one fist is left. That child is the winner and becomes the new leader. It can also be used for picking teams – each time the one fist is left, the child goes in one or other team, thus ensuring fair selection.

1 onion, peeled and diced

1 carrot, peeled and diced

2–3 stalks celery, finely chopped

2 kumara, peeled and diced

3 cups chicken or vegetable or fish stock (or water)

535-gram can Wattie's Very Special Pumpkin and Vegetable Soup

450-gram packet Sealord Simply Natural Dory Fillets

1 cup cream or lite cream

½ cup chopped fresh celery or parsley leaves

very special fish chowder

serves 4–6

preparation time **15 minutes** cooking time **30 minutes**

Cook the onion, carrot and celery in a dash of oil in a large saucepan over a moderately high heat for 3–4 minutes until just lightly browned.

Add the kumara, stock or water and can of soup and simmer for 10 minutes until the vegetables are tender.

Add the frozen fillets and heat, without simmering, for 10–12 minutes until the fish fillets are cooked. As they cook, gently break the fillets into chunky pieces with a spoon. Stir in the cream but do not boil.

Season with the celery or parsley leaves before serving.

allyson's tip

If you would like a thicker chowder, mix 1 tablespoon of cornflour with a little water to make a smooth paste. Stir in with the celery leaves and cook for one minute until the soup thickens.

allyson's tip

Celery leaves have a most delicious fresh flavour and are just wonderful tossed into salads, pasta dishes or hearty casseroles and soups. Don't discard them — keep them lightly rinsed in a plastic bag in the fridge to remain fresh.

did you know

The potato produces more nutritious food, more quickly, on less land and in harsher climates than any other major crop.

1 large red onion, peeled and sliced

4 stalks celery, trimmed and sliced

1 tablespoon minced garlic

1 teaspoon celery seeds (optional)

300 grams salami, finely sliced

2 large, waxy potatoes, peeled and finely diced

425-gram can Craig's Kidney Beans, well-drained

400-gram can Wattie's Tomatoes Chopped with Roasted Garlic and Onion

1 litre chicken stock

½ cup roughly chopped fresh celery or parsley leaves

salami and bean soup

serves 4–5

preparation time **15 minutes** cooking time **20 minutes**

In a large saucepan heat a dash of oil and cook the red onion, celery and garlic for 2–3 minutes until just fragrant.

Add the celery seeds if you have them, with the salami, potatoes, kidney beans, tomatoes and stock.

Simmer gently for 15 minutes. Season with pepper to taste and finish with the freshly chopped or torn celery or parsley leaves. Serve with plenty of toasted crusty bread.

allyson's tips

- To make a quick basil paste, process 1 cup fresh basil leaves, 2–3 tablespoons olive oil and 2 tablespoons grated cheese. Alternatively use Gourmet Garden Basil or Basil Pesto.

- A bouquet garni is prepared from a bay leaf and a few sprigs of parsley and thyme, tied together with string.

- If using bought dried pre-mixed bouquet garni, use sparingly as they can be strong if not overpowering.

400-gram can Craig's Cannellini Beans, rinsed and well-drained

2 carrots, peeled and diced

250-gram piece pumpkin, peeled and diced

2 large waxy potatoes, peeled and diced

1 onion, peeled and diced

1 leek, trimmed, washed and diced

½ cup broken spaghetti pasta

1 bouquet garni (optional)

2½ litres water or chicken stock

400-gram can Wattie's Chopped Tomatoes or

4 large tomatoes blanched and chopped

1–2 handfuls sliced green beans or 2 courgettes, trimmed and diced

1 cup Wattie's Frozen Baby Peas

2 tablespoons basil paste

country vegetable soup with basil

serves 6

preparation time **20 minutes** cooking time **25 minutes**

Place the cannellini beans in a saucepan with the carrots, pumpkin, potatoes, onion, leek, spaghetti, bouquet garni and water or chicken stock and bring slowly to a gentle simmer. Simmer gently for 15 minutes.

Add the tomatoes, beans or courgettes, and peas and simmer a further 5 minutes.

Remove the bouquet garni, season and stir in the basil paste and serve immediately. Do not reheat.

salads

allyson's tip

Potatoes are best stored
with whatever dirt remains
clinging to them.

did you know

Candied sweet potatoes are
a traditional accompaniment
to Thanksgiving turkey in
many states of America.

In Creole cookery they are
whipped into creams or
made into soufflés.

500 grams kumara, peeled and cut into bite-sized pieces

1 lime, grated rind and juice

1 avocado, halved, stoned, peeled and diced

425-gram can Craig's Kidney Beans in brine, drained and rinsed

1 cup cherry tomatoes, halved

2 cups torn spinach leaves

170-gram pottle Wattie's Frozen Guacamole or Mexican Guacomole, defrosted

2 tablespoons sour cream

2 tablespoons chopped fresh coriander

mexican kumara and bean salad

serves 4

preparation time **15 minutes** cooking time **15 minutes**

Cook the kumara in boiling salted water until tender. Drain and cool thoroughly. Dice the kumara and toss with the lime rind and juice.

Place the kumara in a serving dish, scatter over the avocado, kidney beans, cherry tomatoes and spinach.

Mix together the guacamole and sour cream. Spoon over the kumara salad and toss gently to combine. Garnish with chopped coriander.

allyson's tips

- Always peel potatoes as thinly as possible as many of the vitamins are concentrated just under the skin.

- If you do not have any dill and lemon seasoning, substitute 1 tablespoon chopped fresh, or 1 teaspoon dried, dill and the grated rind of one lemon, along with a sprinkling of salt and pepper.

500 grams kumara, peeled
and cut into bite-sized
pieces

1–2 stalks celery, thinly
sliced

1–2 teaspoons capers,
rinsed and chopped

1 lemon, grated rind

2–3 spring onions, trimmed
and chopped

1 teaspoon Gregg's Dill and
Lemon Seasoning

1–2 tablespoons chopped
fresh dill (optional)

½ cup Eta Sour Cream and
Chives Dressing

kumara, lemon, and dill salad

serves 4

preparation time **15 minutes** cooking time **15 minutes**

Cook the kumara in boiling salted
water until just tender. Drain and cool.

Place the kumara in a serving dish,
add the celery, capers, lemon rind and
spring onions.

Mix together the dill and lemon
seasoning, fresh dill (if using) and sour
cream and chives dressing. Pour over
the kumara salad and toss gently to
combine. Garnish with a little chopped
dill.

allyson's tip

Often in British cookbooks, you will find new potatoes are called Chats. These are small new potatoes. Here substitute Jersey Bennies or similar.

did you know

International potato names:
· Spain and Italy – patata
· Finland – peruna
· France – pomme de terre
· Germany – kartoffel

· Holland – aardappel
· India – aloo
· Wales – taten
· Indonesia – kentang

500 grams new potatoes, scrubbed and diced

2 spring onions, trimmed and sliced

2 stalks celery, sliced

1 green capsicum, thinly sliced

½ cup Eta Classic Mayonnaise

2 tablespoons horseradish cream

2 tablespoons chopped fresh chives

spring potato salad

serves 4–6

preparation time **10 minutes** cooking time **10 minutes**

Cook the potatoes in boiling salted water until tender. Drain and cool.

Place the potatoes in a serving dish and scatter over the spring onions, celery and green capsicum.

Mix the mayonnaise, horseradish and chives together and pour over the potato salad and toss gently to combine. Serve garnished with extra chives if wished.

500 grams new potatoes, scrubbed and cut into bite-sized pieces

1 tablespoon cumin seeds

¼ cup oil

2 tablespoons curry paste (see allyson's tip)

1 red capsicum, finely sliced

2–3 spring onions, trimmed and sliced

1 red chilli, deseeded and finely chopped

¼ cup toasted cashews

2 tablespoons chopped fresh coriander

¼ cup Eta Classic Mayonnaise

2 tablespoons mango chutney

curry and cumin spiked potato salad

serves 4

preparation time **10 minutes** cooking time **15 minutes**

Cook the potatoes in boiling salted water until tender. Drain.

Toast the cumin seeds in a non-stick frying-pan for about 1 minute until fragrant, add the oil and curry paste. Cook a further 1–2 minutes. Add the potatoes and toss to coat. Remove from the heat.

Place the potatoes in a serving bowl, and scatter over the red capsicum, spring onion, chilli, cashews and coriander.

Mix together the mayonnaise and mango chutney. Pour over the potato salad and toss gently to coat. If wished add lettuce leaf greens.

allyson's tip

Vary the flavour of this
salad by using tikka
masala, rogan josh, korma
or vindaloo curry pastes.

did you know

Spanish sailors and
explorers were the first
Europeans to eat the potato
and later introduced them
to Spain in the second half
of the sixteenth century.

500 grams new potatoes, scrubbed and cut into bite-sized pieces

2 chorizo sausages, sliced in half lengthwise

2–3 teaspoons Gregg's Paprika

½ cup Eta Balsamic Vinaigrette

1 red capsicum, chargrilled and sliced

6 semi-dried tomatoes, thinly sliced or 6–8 black olives

150 grams green beans, blanched and halved

1 small red onion, peeled and thinly sliced

spanish potato salad

serves 4–6

preparation time **20 minutes** cooking time **15 minutes**

Cook the potato in boiling salted water for around 15 minutes or until just tender. Drain.

Heat a dash of oil in a non-stick frying-pan. Cook the chorizo sausage 2–3 minutes each side until golden. Remove from the heat and slice.

Add the paprika to the pan and cook for only a few seconds. Pour in the vinaigrette and stir to combine. Remove from the heat.

Arrange the potatoes on a serving dish and scatter over the red capsicum, chorizo, semi-dried tomatoes or olives, green beans and onion. Pour over the warm dressing and toss gently to combine. Serve garnished with parsley leaves if wished.

allyson's tip

The flavours in paprika are only released once heated, hence the reason for cooking the paprika in the pan and then mixing with the vinaigrette.

allyson's tips

· If your potatoes have any
green areas, all you need
to do is to peel thickly to
remove. The greening will not
hurt you unless you eat an

awful lot of it, but it is prudent
to remove the green area.

· If you do not have salami
sticks use 100 grams sliced

salami or 4 rashers bacon,
grilled until crispy and
crumbled.

500 grams new potatoes, peeled and cut into even-sized pieces

1 small red onion, peeled and sliced

4 small salami sticks, sliced

¼ cup black olives

390-gram can artichoke hearts, drained and halved

2 tablespoons toasted pine nuts

2 tablespoons torn fresh basil leaves

2–3 juicy tomatoes, cut into wedges (optional)

½ cup Eta Lite and Free French Dressing

½–1 teaspoon minced garlic

potato and artichoke salad

serves 4–6

preparation time **20 minutes** cooking time **15 minutes**

Cook the potatoes in boiling salted water until just tender. Drain and cool.

Place the potatoes in a serving dish, add the onion, salami, olives, artichoke, pine nuts, basil and tomatoes if using.

Mix the vinaigrette and garlic together and pour over the salad. Toss gently to combine. Garnish with a few more basil leaves and season well with pepper.

500-gram bag Wattie's Frozen Broad Beans

½ 750-gram bag Wattie's Frozen Whole Baby Beans

1 lettuce

4 tomatoes, cut into eighths

10 cooked baby new potatoes, halved

4 hard-boiled eggs, peeled and quartered

12 black olives

180-gram can Greenseas Tuna in Water, drained

½ cup Wattie's Classic Mayonnaise

¼ cup finely chopped fresh herbs (such as parsley, chives or basil)

2 tablespoons water

french salad

serves 5–6

preparation time **20 minutes** cooking time **10 minutes**

Blanch the broad and baby beans in boiling water for 2 minutes. Refresh in cold water, drain well. Peel the broad beans if wished.

Wash and drain the lettuce leaves. Cut or tear into large pieces and arrange on a large platter.

Carefully arrange the beans, tomatoes, potatoes, eggs and olives on top.

Place chunks of tuna evenly over the top of the salad.

For the dressing mix together the mayonnaise, herbs and water and spoon over the salad.

allyson's tip

I roll the beetroot on a few pieces of absorbent paper before halving and placing on the salad. This helps prevent the beetroot bleeding onto the other salad ingredients.

6 spicy beef or pork
   sausages
½ 750-gram bag Wattie's
   Frozen Whole Baby Beans
1 lettuce
4 tomatoes, diced
10 cooked baby new
   potatoes, halved
1 each red and green
   capsicum, thinly sliced
820-gram can Wattie's
   Whole Baby Beetroot,
   well drained

sweet orange dressing
¼ cup each orange juice,
   honey, oil and cider
   vinegar
¼ cup chopped fresh
   herbs (chives, parsley,
   marjoram, basil or a mix
   of each)

russian salad

serves 4
preparation time **20 minutes** cooking time **10 minutes**

Cook the sausages in a frying-pan or under the grill. Cool and then slice diagonally.

Blanch the baby beans and refresh in cold water. Drain well on absorbent paper.

Wash and drain the lettuce. Arrange the leaves in a large salad bowl or on a platter.

Sprinkle over the beans, tomatoes, potatoes and capsicum.

Halve any large beetroot and arrange neatly on top of the salad with the sliced sausage. Pour over the dressing and serve.

sweet orange dressing
Whisk all ingredients together until smooth.

light meals

8 Wattie's Frozen Mashed
   Potato patties or 1 cup
   soft mashed potatoes
2–3 rashers rindless
   bacon, diced
1½ cups self-raising flour
¼ teaspoon baking soda
¼ cup grated Parmesan

2 tablespoons chopped
   fresh parsley or Gourmet
   Garden Parsley
2 eggs, lightly beaten
¼ cup milk
2 tablespoons additional
   grated Parmesan

potato and
bacon scones

serves 12–16
preparation time **10 minutes** cooking time **12–15 minutes**

Cook the potato patties (if using) covered in a microwave for 5 minutes. Stir until smooth and leave to cool.

Pan-fry the bacon until crisp.

Sift the flour and baking soda together into a bowl. Gently mix through the potatoes, bacon, Parmesan and parsley, and make a well in the centre.

Beat the egg and milk together and pour into the well. Use a knife to mix to a soft dough. Add more milk if necessary (the amount of milk required depends on the softness of the mashed potato).

Turn the dough onto a lightly floured surface. Knead lightly until smooth, roll or pat out to about 2.5 cm–3-cm thickness and cut into 4-cm circles or squares.

Transfer to a baking paper-covered oven tray. Brush the tops with a little milk and sprinkle the extra Parmesan evenly over the scones.

Bake towards the top of a 220 °C oven for 12–15 minutes until well risen and golden brown.

Serve warm and lightly buttered.

did you know

In the Andes 'heritage potatoes', called 'gift potatoes', are still grown by local farmers. These potatoes are rarely sold, instead they are offered as gifts to prestigious guests or used in ceremonial dinners.

3 rashers rindless
   bacon, diced

3 spring onions, trimmed
   and sliced

750 grams starchy
   potatoes, cooked,
   mashed and cooled

2 tablespoons chopped
   fresh parsley

1 egg, lightly beaten

About ¼ cup flour for
   coating

170-gram pottle Wattie's
   Frozen Guacamole,
   defrosted

irish potato and bacon cakes

serves 4–6
preparation time **10 minutes** cooking time **10 minutes**

Heat a dash of oil in a non-stick pan and cook the bacon and spring onion until the bacon is crispy. Cool.

Mix together the mashed potato, bacon, spring onion, parsley and egg. Season well with salt and pepper. Shape into 10–12 patties and toss lightly in flour.

Heat a dash of oil, or a knob of butter, in a non-stick frying-pan and cook the potato cakes for 6–8 minutes, turning once until golden brown and hot.

Serve with guacamole and your favourite brunch foods like grilled bacon, tomato and sausages.

allyson's tip

Left-over cold mashed potato can be used to thicken soups and casseroles or can be made into a variety of flavoured potato cakes.

did you know

During the Irish potato famine in the mid-nineteenth century and in particular during 1845–1848, about 1 million Irish people died of disease and starvation. And about 1¼ million people emigrated from Ireland and settled around the world, chiefly in the USA.

allyson's tips

- Light will turn potatoes green and warmth and moisture will help cause potatoes to sprout and shrivel, hastening rotting. Store potatoes in a dark, cool place with ample air circulation. Try a cool airy laundry or garage.

- All-purpose potatoes, or floury potatoes are suited for baking whole and stuffing. See page 9.

- Microwave cooking time will vary depending on the variety and size of the potato, and the wattage of your microwave. Treat microwave cooking times as a guide only.

6 even-shaped, medium-sized starchy potatoes

180-gram can Greenseas Tuna in Oil, drained if wished

10–12 semi-dried or sun-dried tomatoes

2 chargrilled red capsicums, diced

100 grams marinated feta, crumbled

½ cup grated cheese (Mozzarella or Edam or similar)

1 tablespoon capers, rinsed and chopped

2 tablespoons fresh sage or oregano leaves, or 2 teaspoons Gregg's Rubbed Sage or Oregano

tuscan crumble-topped baked potatoes

serves 6

preparation time **15 minutes** cooking time **1 hour**

Wash the potatoes and dry well with a paper towel. Rub the potatoes with oil and sprinkle with salt if wished.

Bake at 190 °C for 45 minutes until the potatoes are tender.

Toss together the tuna, tomatoes, capsicums, feta, cheese, capers and herbs.

When the potatoes are cooked cut a shallow lid out of the centre and divide the filling among the potatoes.

Return to the oven for 10–12 minutes or until the filling is hot and the cheese is beginning to melt.

Serve with a crispy green salad.

'My idea of heaven is a great big baked potato and someone to share it with' – Oprah Winfrey

1 kilogram even-sized
    baking potatoes,
    scrubbed
¼ cup olive oil or melted
    butter
125 grams feta, finely
    crumbled
85-gram pouch Greenseas
    Oven Dried Tomato and
    Basil Tuna

2 tablespoons finely
    chopped fresh oregano or
    1 teaspoon Gregg's Dried
    Oregano
¼ cup grated cheese

oregano and feta-topped baked potato

serves 4
preparation time **15 minutes** cooking time **1 hour**

Prick the potatoes and bake at 190 °C for 50 minutes or until tender. Allow to cool.

Toss together the olive oil, feta, flaked tuna and oregano and season with pepper.

Slice the tops off the potatoes and carefully scoop out the soft potato centre and mix with the feta and tuna mixture. Spoon back into the potatoes, piling up if necessary.

Place in an ovenproof dish on a baking paper-lined tray. Scatter over the grated cheese.

Bake at 190 °C for 10 minutes or until hot and golden.

'What I say is that, if a fellow likes potatoes, he must be a pretty decent sort of fellow' – A.A. Milne

4 large baking potatoes,
    washed

150 grams lean pork mince

2 spring onions, trimmed
    and finely sliced

½ cup Wattie's Frozen
    Supersweet Corn

½ cup Wattie's Sweet and
    Sour Sauce

sweet and sour pork stuffed potatoes

serves 4
preparation time **10 minutes** cooking time **35 minutes**

Prick the potatoes and place evenly spaced on a microwave-proof plate. Microwave on high power (100%) for 12–14 minutes or until the potatoes are tender. Alternatively rub the potatoes in a little oil and place on a baking tray. Bake at 190 °C for 45 minutes until cooked.

Brown the pork mince in a frying-pan in a dash of oil over a high heat. Stir in the spring onion, corn and sweet and sour sauce. Stir together and remove from the heat.

Slice the tops off the potatoes. Scoop out the filling and mix with the pork mixture. Refill the potatoes, piling the mixture up. Place on a baking paper-lined oven tray.

Bake at 200 °C for 15 minutes until piping hot and golden.

4 medium-sized starchy
  potatoes, scrubbed

2–3 spring onions, trimmed
  and finely chopped

1 red chilli, deseeded and
  finely chopped

1 teaspoon minced ginger

2–3 tablespoons Malay
  curry paste

¼ cup sour cream

¼ cup chopped fresh
  coriander or Gourmet
  Garden Coriander

malay curry paste

2 red chillies, deseeded and
  finely chopped

3 shallots, finely chopped

1 teaspoon ground
  cardamom

1 teaspoon ground cloves

2 tablespoons ground cumin

2 tablespoons ground
  coriander

2 tablespoons turmeric

½ cup Wattie's Tomato Paste

½ cup oil

malay curry baked potatoes

serves 4

preparation time **15 minutes** cooking time **1¼ hours**

Rub the potato skins with a little oil. Bake at 190 °C for 1 hour until tender.

Heat a dash of oil in a non-stick pan and cook the spring onions, chilli and ginger for 2–3 minutes until tender. Add the curry paste and cook a further 1 minute. Add the sour cream and stir gently to combine.

Cut the top off each potato and carefully scoop out most of the flesh. Mash the flesh and add the spring onion mixture. Stir gently to combine.

Return the filling to the potato, piling up if necessary. Return to the oven for 10 minutes until reheated.

Serve garnished with chopped fresh coriander.

malay curry paste

Heat a dash of oil in a frying-pan, add the chillies and shallots and cook over a gentle heat for 7–8 minutes until the shallots are tender.

Add the spices and cook a further 1–2 minutes until fragrant. Increase the heat and stir in the tomato paste and cook for a further 2–3 minutes until it darkens to a deep red colour. Add the remaining oil and salt to season, and stir to combine well.

Keep in an airtight container and refrigerate or freeze.

allyson's tips

· When making this paste, use a flavourless oil such as canola or light olive oil.

· If you don't have time to make the curry paste from scratch, a store-bought product can be used.

did you know

Around 500,000 tonnes of the humble spud are grown annually in New Zealand. As an average potato is 175 grams, that means we grow 2,855,000,000 potatoes per year! Potatoes provide New Zealanders with around 30% of their vitamin C requirement.

4 even-sized kumara, washed

400 grams lean lamb mince

2 tablespoons tikka masala
curry paste

2 teaspoons minced garlic

1 tablespoon minced ginger

2 large, juicy tomatoes,
very finely chopped or ½
400-gram can Wattie's
Chopped Tomatoes

2 tablespoons chopped
fresh coriander

¼ cup grated cheese

tikka masala curry paste

2 teaspoons cumin seeds

2 tablespoons oil

1 tablespoon minced ginger

2 teaspoons minced garlic

1 teaspoon ground coriander

1 teaspoon ground turmeric

½ teaspoon garam masala

¼ cup Wattie's Tomato Paste

1 teaspoon sugar

½ teaspoon salt

2 teaspoons grated
lemon rind

2 tablespoons lemon juice

tikka masala baked kumara

serves 4
preparation time **15 minutes** cooking time **1 hour**

Rub a little oil on the kumara and bake at 190 °C for 40–50 minutes until tender.

Heat a dash of oil in a frying-pan and brown the mince over a high heat. When brown add curry paste, garlic and ginger and cook for a further minute.

Add the tomatoes and simmer for 10 minutes until the mixture is thick.

Slice the top off each kumara and scoop the cooked kumara into a bowl. Add the mince and coriander and mix together roughly. Return the filling to the kumara shells and then sprinkle each with a little grated cheese.

Return to the oven for 10 minutes or until golden.

tikka masala curry paste
Toast the cumin seeds in a non-stick pan until fragrant. Add the oil and when hot add the ginger, garlic, coriander, turmeric and garam masala. Cook a further minute. Add the tomato paste, sugar and salt. Cook until the tomato turns a rich red colour. Remove from the heat and stir in the lemon rind and juice.

Keep in an airtight container and refrigerate or freeze.

allyson's tips

- Vary this recipe by using beef or chicken mince, or for a vegetarian option, roughly mash a 425-gram can of Craig's Kidney or Cannellini Beans and use in place of the meat.

- If you don't have time to make the curry paste from scratch, a store-bought product can be used.

allyson's tip

When I bake potatoes or
kumara at home I always
rub them with oil and a little
salt before baking. This
gives them a delicious crispy
tangy baked outer skin.

did you know

Yams are not related to the
potato, they are a different
plant species altogether.

- 4 medium-sized orange or golden kumara
- 234-gram can crushed pineapple, well drained
- 1 teaspoon minced fresh ginger (optional)
- 2–3 spring onions, trimmed and chopped
- 340-gram can Hellaby's Corned Beef
- ½ cup grated cheese (Edam or Colby)

tropical baked kumara

serves 4–5
preparation time **10 minutes** cooking time **1 hour**

Wash the kumara and dry well. Trim the ends and rub with a little oil if wished. Place on a baking tray.

Bake at 200 °C for 40–45 minutes or until well cooked. Alternatively prick the kumara with a fork and microwave on high power for 15 minutes or until tender.

Halve the kumaras lengthwise and scoop the flesh into a bowl.

Add the pineapple, ginger, spring onion and corned beef. Mix gently with a fork to break up the corned beef and mix the ingredients lightly. Do not mash.

Re-fill each kumara with equal amounts of the mixture and return to the baking tray. Sprinkle each with a little grated cheese.

Cook at 200 °C for 15 minutes until piping hot and golden. Serve with your favourite chutney and salad.

4 even-sized kumara,
    washed
2 85-gram pouches
    Greenseas Sweet Thai
    Chilli Tuna, flaked
3 spring onions, trimmed
    and finely chopped
1 red chilli, deseeded and
    finely chopped

1 lime, grated rind and juice
2 tablespoons chopped fresh
    coriander or Gourmet
    Garden Coriander

sweet thai chilli tuna baked kumara

serves 4
preparation time **10 minutes** cooking time **1 hour**

Rub the kumara skins with a little olive
oil. Bake at 190 °C for 40–50 minutes
until tender.

Cut the top off each kumara and
carefully scoop out the flesh. Mash the
flesh, add the tuna, spring onion, chilli,
lime rind and juice and coriander. Stir
gently to combine.

Return the filling to the kumara, piling
up as required and place on an oven
tray. Return to the oven for 10 minutes
or until piping hot.

Serve garnished with coriander and
accompany with lime wedges and
your favourite sweet chilli sauce.

4 even-sized baking
  potatoes, scrubbed and
  rinsed

420 grams Wattie's Lite
  Spaghetti

75 grams sliced ham,
  chopped

2 tablespoons chopped
  fresh chives

3 tablespoons grated cheese

spaghetti and cheese stuffed potatoes

serves 4
preparation time **10 minutes** cooking time **30 minutes**

Prick the potatoes and microwave
for 12–15 minutes until tender.
Alternatively bake at 200 °C for about
1 hour until tender. Cool.

Slice the tops off the potatoes. Scoop
out the centres and combine with the
spaghetti, ham and chives. Fill the
potatoes and sprinkle with the grated
cheese. Return to the baking tray.

Bake at 200 °C for 15 minutes until
piping hot and golden.

allyson's tip

To bake potatoes more quickly, pierce through the centre with a potato nail (available at cook shops) or a clean long nail. The nail will help the potato cook from the inside out.

4 even-sized baking
  potatoes, scrubbed

400 grams lean beef or
  lamb mince

2 teaspoons minced garlic

3 spring onions, trimmed
  and chopped

½ cup HP Sauce

¼ cup water or beef stock

½ cup chopped prunes
  or raisins

2 tablespoons grated cheese

2 tablespoons chopped
  fresh parsley or chives

HP baked potatoes

serves 4

preparation time **10 minutes** cooking time **1¼ hours**

Prick the potatoes with a fork. Bake at 190 °C for 1 hour until tender.

Heat a dash of oil in a non-stick pan and brown the mince over a high heat. Add the garlic and spring onion to the pan and cook for 1–2 minutes before returning the mince to the pan with the HP sauce, water or stock and prunes or raisins. Cook for 5 minutes stirring regularly.

Cut the top off each potato and carefully scoop out most of the flesh. Coarsely mash the flesh and mix with the mince. Return the filling to the potato, piling up as high as necessary. Top with the grated cheese.

Return to the oven for about 10 minutes and bake until golden brown and hot. Serve garnished with chopped parsley or chives.

4 baking potatoes, scrubbed

200 grams Tegel chicken
   bacon rashers, diced

3 spring onions, trimmed
   and sliced

170-gram pottle Wattie's
   Frozen Mexican
   Guacamole, defrosted

¼ cup sour cream

½ cup cherry tomatoes,
   halved or quartered

mexican chicken bacon baked potatoes

serves 4

preparation time **10 minutes** cooking time **1 hour**

Prick the potatoes with a fork. Rub with a little oil and salt if wished and place on a baking tray or in a baking dish.

Bake at 190 °C for 1 hour or until tender.

Heat a dash of oil in a non-stick pan and cook the chicken bacon and spring onions until golden.

Cut the top off each potato and carefully scoop out most of the flesh. Coarsely mash the flesh and add the chicken bacon, spring onion, avocado, sour cream and most of the cherry tomatoes. Stir gently to combine.

Refill the potatoes while hot and serve garnished with remaining tomatoes and a little coriander if wished.

allyson's tip

500 grams of potatoes will
yield approximately 2 cups
mashed potatoes – sufficient
to feed 4–5 people.

750 grams kumara, peeled and chopped

1 small onion, peeled and finely chopped

1 teaspoon Gregg's Curry Powder

227-gram can crushed pineapple in juice, very well drained

1 egg

¼ cup Lea & Perrins Worcestershire Sauce

340-gram can Hellaby's Reduced Fat Corned Beef, chilled

kumara and corned beef hash patties

serves 4–6

preparation time **30 minutes** cooking time **10 minutes**

Cook the kumara in boiling salted water until tender, drain and mash.

Cook the onion in a dash of oil in a frying-pan until soft but not coloured. Add the curry powder and cook for a further minute.

Add the onion to the kumara with the pineapple, egg and Lea & Perrins Worcestershire Sauce and mix well. Flake in the corned beef and fold through gently.

Shape into 8 even-sized patties and pan fry in a little oil for 6–7 minutes until hot and golden, turning once.

Serve topped with a quick salsa prepared from diced tomato, celery and chopped parsley. Accompany with your favourite brunch or lunch ingredients.

500-gram packet Wattie's
   Frozen Golden Heart
   Hash Browns
425-gram can Wattie's
   Baked Beans
4 eggs
4 rashers bacon, finely sliced
¾ cup grated cheese (Edam,
   Colby, etc.)

baked bean hash

serves 6
preparation time **20 minutes** cooking time **30 minutes**

Place the hash browns in the base of a large baking dish, trimming where necessary.

Pour over the baked beans and spread out evenly.

Beat the eggs together and pour over the top of the baked beans.

Sprinkle the bacon and cheese over the top of the eggs, and season with pepper if wished.

Bake at 200 °C towards the top of the oven for 30 minutes until set. Stand for 2 minutes before serving. Garnish with chopped parsley if wished and serve in wedges.

allyson's tips

- Red-skinned kumara are best used in this recipe.
- Beating the egg white ensures light, fluffy fritters.

82

410-gram can Wattie's
    Cream Style Corn

2 teaspoons minced ginger

2 tablespoons chopped
    fresh herbs (thyme or
    chives)

½ cup self-raising flour

¼ cup milk

1 egg, separated

½ cup roughly mashed
    cooked cold kumara

kumara and corn fritters

serves 4

preparation time **15 minutes** cooking time **15 minutes**

In a bowl mix together the corn,
ginger, herbs, self-raising flour, milk
and egg yolk.

In a clean bowl beat the egg white
until stiff. Fold the egg white and
kumara into the corn mixture.

Heat a little butter or oil in a non-stick
frying-pan and cook large spoonfuls
over a low to moderate heat for about
3 minutes each side. Serve with your
favourite brunch ingredients.

main course

1 onion, peeled and finely chopped

2–3 teaspoons minced garlic

100 grams salami, diced

1 tablespoon Gregg's Paprika

1 tablespoon flour

1 tablespoon sugar

2 tablespoons Wattie's Tomato Paste

400-gram can Wattie's Tomatoes with Roasted Garlic and Onion

½ cup chicken stock

750 grams waxy potatoes, peeled and thinly sliced

1 cup grated cheese

hungarian potato hot pot

serves 6

preparation time **30 minutes** cooking time **1–1¼ hours**

Heat a dash of oil in a frying-pan and cook the onion, garlic and salami until the onion is soft.

Add the paprika and cook only until fragrant. Stir in the flour, sugar and tomato paste and cook for 2 minutes, stirring well until the mixture has darkened in colour before stirring in the chopped tomatoes and chicken stock. Set aside.

Arrange half of the potatoes in the base of a 7–8-cup-capacity lasagne-style dish.

Spread over the tomato mixture, then top with the remaining sliced potatoes. Scatter over the cheese.

Bake at 180 °C for 1–1¼ hours or until potatoes are tender. Serve with a crispy salad.

500 grams casseroling lamb, diced into 2–3-cm cubes

1 onion, peeled and sliced

2–3 teaspoons Gourmet Garden Garlic

3 cups chicken stock

2 lemons, grated rind and juice

1 tablespoon chopped fresh thyme

3 tablespoons rolled oats

750-gram bag Wattie's Frozen Winter Vegetables Recipe Mix

spiced lamb with potatoes and lemon

serves 4

preparation time **30 minutes** cooking time **1½ hours**

Heat a dash of oil in a lidded frying-pan or flameproof casserole and brown the meat over a high heat. This may be best done in two batches. Set the meat aside.

Add the onion and garlic to the pan and cook until brown. Add the chicken stock, lemon rind and juice and chopped thyme to the pan.

Return the meat to the casserole and cover.

Bake at 160 °C for 1 hour. Stir in the oats and the chunky vegetables and return the casserole to the oven for a further 30 minutes until the vegetables and meat are tender.

Serve with broad beans, if wished, and garnish with fresh thyme and accompany with plenty of crusty bread to mop up the juices.

'Money is the root of all evil, and yet it is such a useful root that we cannot get on without it any more than we can without potatoes.'
– Louisa May Alcott (1832–1888), American novelist

1 onion, peeled and finely
 sliced

2 teaspoons minced garlic

1 tablespoon yellow or
 brown mustard seeds

405-gram can Wattie's Rich
 Tomato Butter Chicken

400-gram can Wattie's
 Indian Style Tomatoes

½ cup water

750 grams new potatoes,
 scrubbed and diced

4–5 cups well-packed torn
 spinach leaves

½ cup cream

¼ cup chopped fresh
 coriander

fresh mango chutney

1 mango, peeled and diced

¼ red onion, peeled and
 very finely chopped

2–4 tablespoons finely
 chopped fresh coriander

1 teaspoon minced ginger

1 lemon, juice

potato and mustard seed curry

serves 4–5

preparation time **15 minutes** cooking time **35–40 minutes**

Heat a dash of oil in a non-stick lidded frying-pan or large saucepan and cook the onion, garlic and mustard seeds for 3–4 minutes until the mustard seeds begin to pop.

Add the butter chicken sauce, tomatoes, water and potatoes. Simmer for 20–25 minutes until the potatoes are tender, stirring occasionally.

Add the spinach and cream and heat only until the spinach has wilted. Stir in the coriander. Serve immediately garnished with fresh mango chutney, if wished. Accompany with naan bread or poppadoms.

Fresh Mango Chutney
Toss ingredients together.

4 large starchy potatoes, peeled

a hearty knob of butter

¼ cup milk

350–500 grams smoked fish fillets, flaked

3 hard-boiled eggs, peeled

535-gram can Wattie's Very Special Kumara and Vegetable or Pumpkin and Vegetable Soup

½ cup cream

2 cups Wattie's Frozen Chuckwagon Corn

¼ cup chopped fresh parsley

½ cup grated cheese (e.g. Parmesan, Edam, Colby, Cheddar)

cheesy potato-topped smoked fish pie

serves 4
preparation time **20 minutes** cooking time **45 minutes**

Cook the potatoes in plenty of boiling salted water until tender. Drain and mash with the butter and sufficient milk until smooth. Season with salt and pepper to taste if wished.

Flake the fish into a large bowl, discarding any bones. Cut the eggs into quarters and add to the fish with the soup, cream, frozen vegetables and chopped parsley.

Spoon the mixture into a 6–8-cup capacity ovenproof dish.

Top with the mashed potatoes and sprinkle over the grated cheese.

Bake at 200 °C for 30–35 minutes until piping hot and golden. Serve with your favourite vegetables.

allyson's tip

Avoid potatoes that have
wrinkled or wilted skins
— they are well past
their prime.

95

- 1 cup of grated cheddar-style cheese is approximately 100 grams.
- 300 grams of kumara is approximately 1 medium–large kumara.

750 grams all-purpose
    potatoes, well scrubbed
300 grams orange-fleshed
    kumara, well scrubbed
4 rashers rindless bacon,
    diced
1 medium leek, trimmed and
    thinly sliced

420-gram can Wattie's
    Creamy Chicken
    Condensed Soup
½ cup cream
2 teaspoons Gregg's Curry
    Powder
1 cup grated cheese

Peas

Ham

baked cheesy potato and kumara layer

serves 6

preparation time **20 minutes** cooking time **40–45 minutes**

Parboil the potatoes and kumara, in their skins for 10 minutes. Drain and slice the potatoes into half-centimetre slices. Cool the kumara, peel and slice into half-centimetre slices.

Heat a dash of oil in a frying-pan and cook the bacon until crispy. Add the leek and cook for 2–3 minutes until tender but not brown. Mix the soup, cream and curry powder together in a bowl and season with pepper.

Layer the potatoes, kumara, leek, bacon and soup mixture in an 8-cup capacity ovenproof dish, finishing with a layer of soup. Scatter over the grated cheese.

Bake at 180 °C for 40–45 minutes until the potatoes are tender and the top is golden.

Serve with a crispy salad as a main course or as an accompaniment to a meal.

allyson's tip

Where possible, leave the
skin on the potatoes when
cooking. It adds fibre,
nutrients and texture.

2 tablespoons Gregg's Paprika

1 teaspoon Gregg's Curry Powder

1 teaspoon fennel seeds, crushed

½ teaspoon salt

¼ teaspoon ground cardamom or ginger

¼ teaspoon ground cinnamon

1 onion, peeled and diced

3 cups vegetable stock, or stock and water combined

1 cup red or brown lentils, washed

750 grams waxy potatoes, washed and cut into chunks

4 cooked chorizo sausages, sliced

750-gram bag Wattie's Frozen Chunky Mix

¼ cup chopped fresh parsley

potato and red lentil curry

serves 4
preparation time **15 minutes** cooking time **35–40 minutes**

Mix the paprika, curry powder, fennel seeds, salt, ground cardamom or ginger and cinnamon together.

Cook the onion in a deep-lidded frying-pan in 3–4 tablespoons oil until lightly brown. Add the ground spices and cook 1–2 minutes or until fragrant.

Stir in the vegetable stock and lentils and simmer very gently uncovered for 10 minutes.

Add the potatoes, cover and cook a further 10 minutes. Add the chorizo and chunky vegetables. Cook a further 10–15 minutes or until the vegetables are tender. Add water if required to make a thinner sauce if wished. Add the chopped parsley.

1 onion, peeled and finely
  chopped

1 each red and green
  capsicum, diced

2 teaspoons minced ginger

1–2 fresh green chillies,
  deseeded and finely
  chopped

1 teaspoon minced garlic

410-gram can Wattie's
  Korma Curry Sauce

400-millilitre can coconut
  milk or cream

750 grams waxy potatoes,
  diced (peeled if wished)

200 grams green beans,
  trimmed and sliced

½–1 cup peanuts, toasted
  and roughly chopped

2 tablespoons chopped
  fresh coriander

potato and roasted peanut curry

serves 4

preparation time **10 minutes** cooking time **35–40 minutes**

Heat a dash of oil in a heavy-based pan and gently cook the onion, capsicums, ginger, chillies and garlic for 3–5 minutes until just softened.

Pour over the curry sauce, coconut milk or cream, add the potatoes and cover.

Simmer very gently for about 15–20 minutes until the potatoes are just tender, stirring often to prevent sticking.

Add the beans and cook a further 5 minutes. Stir in the peanuts and coriander and serve immediately with your favourite Indian chutneys and naan bread or poppadoms.

500 grams casseroling lamb, diced

2 tablespoons olive oil

2 teaspoons ground allspice

2 teaspoons ground cumin

2 teaspoons minced garlic

1 each red and green capsicum, diced

400-gram can Wattie's Tomatoes with Roasted Garlic and Onion

290-gram can Wattie's Tomato Puree

1 cup unsweetened thick yoghurt

¼ cup torn fresh mint leaves

turkish mashed potatoes

450-gram bag Wattie's Frozen Mashed Potato

1 teaspoon cumin seeds, toasted or ½ teaspoon ground cumin

1 teaspoon minced garlic

2 tablespoons chopped fresh parsley or 1 tablespoon dried parsley

turkish lamb with turkish mashed potatoes

serves 4

preparation time **30 minutes** cooking time **1 hour**

Place the lamb, olive oil, allspice, cumin and garlic in a snaplock plastic bag or shallow dish. Toss to coat. Set aside for 15 minutes.

Heat a dash of oil in a lidded frying-pan or flameproof casserole and brown the meat over a high heat.

Add the capsicums and cook a further 2 minutes.

Add the chopped tomatoes and tomato puree, stir and cover.

Bake at 160 °C for 45 minutes until the lamb is tender. Stir in the yoghurt and serve with the turkish mashed potatoes, garnished with the mint.

turkish mashed potatoes
Place the potato patties in a microwave-proof dish and cover. Microwave on high power (100%) for 6 minutes or until piping hot.

Cook the cumin seeds and garlic in a dash of oil until fragrant and the seeds are toasted. Stir in the hot mashed potato and parsley and serve. (If using ground cumin, be careful not to burn it when cooking with the garlic.)

allyson's tips

- Potatoes are so rich in starch they rank as the world's fourth most important food crop, after maize, wheat and rice.

- For casseroling lamb, use well-trimmed diced boneless shoulder.

allyson's tips

· Handle potatoes gently as they bruise easily.

· When buying beef or lamb, look for the Quality Mark logo, which identifies quality New Zealand beef or lamb. Meat with the logo has been trimmed of excess fat and meets the National Heart Foundation's Pick the Tick guidelines.

8–10 lamb shoulder chops, trimmed

1 large onion, peeled and sliced

2 teaspoons minced garlic

2 bay leaves

4 cups chicken or vegetable stock or water

750-gram bag Wattie's Frozen Chunky Casserole Recipe Mix

about ¼ cup Lea & Perrins Worcestershire Sauce

2 tablespoons chopped fresh parsley

country lamb casserole

serves 4–5

preparation time **20 minutes** cooking time **1½ hours**

Cut the lamb shoulder chops in half lengthwise. Brown the chops in a hot frying-pan, with a dash of oil, turning once.

Layer the browned lamb, onion, garlic and bay leaves in a deep casserole or large saucepan, pour over the stock or water.

Cover and simmer gently on top of the stove or cook in the oven at 160 °C for 1 hour.

Add the frozen vegetables and continue cooking or return to the oven for a further 30 minutes until the vegetables are hot and cooked through.

Season with the Worcestershire sauce, and pepper if wished.

Serve in wide bowls garnished with the chopped parsley.

2 large orange-fleshed
 kumara, peeled

2 stalks celery, trimmed and
 washed

4 100% New Zealand pork
 loin chops, rind removed

1–2 tablespoons fresh
 thyme leaves or 1
 teaspoon dried thyme

550-gram can Wattie's
 Just Add Sweet Apricot
 Simmer Sauce

½ 250-gram pottle Tararua
 Lite Crème Fraîche
 (optional)

apricot, pork and kumara bake

serves 4
preparation time **15 minutes** cooking time **40 minutes**

Very thinly slice the kumara and celery
and layer in a lasagne-style dish.

Brown the pork chops in a hot frying-
pan and then place on top of the
vegetables. Scatter over the thyme and
pour over the apricot simmer sauce.

Bake at 190 °C for 40 minutes or until
the pork is crispy, golden and tender.

Lift the pork chops from the dish and
gently stir in the crème fraîche if using.

Serve the pork with seasonal
vegetables.

allyson's tip

Substitute crème fraîche with
sour cream in this recipe.

did you know

Sweet potatoes must
be 'cured' (partially
dried) immediately after
harvesting and stored

between 13 °C and 16 °C
to ensure good keeping
quality and flavour.

1 kilogram red-skinned
   kumara, peeled and
   chopped

1 onion, peeled and finely
   chopped

2 teaspoons minced garlic

1 tablespoon minced ginger

2–3 tablespoons Wattie's
   Indian-style curry paste
   (see tip)

400-gram can Craig's
   Cannellini Beans, rinsed
   and drained

¼ cup chopped fresh
   coriander

**spiced yoghurt and
   cucumber raita**

1 cup plain unsweetened
   yoghurt

1 green chilli, diced or
   1 teaspoon minced
   red chilli

2 tablespoons chopped
   fresh mint leaves

½ cucumber, grated or
   sliced

indian-spiced kumara and bean burgers

serves 6

preparation time **20 minutes** cooking time **10 minutes**

Cook the kumara in boiling salted water for 15 minutes or until tender. Drain.

Cook the onion, garlic and ginger in a dash of oil until tender but not brown. Stir in the curry paste and cook for 1–2 minutes. Cool.

Roughly mash the kumara with the beans and combine with the cooked onion mixture. Season well with salt and pepper. Stir in the fresh coriander. With damp hands shape the mixture into 6 large or 8–12 small patties.

Cook the patties in a little oil over a gentle heat for 3–4 minutes each side or until hot and golden. Serve the patties in warm naan bread with the spiced yoghurt and cucumber raita, and your favourite salad ingredients.

spiced yoghurt and cucumber raita
Mix all the ingredients together.

allyson's tip

Vary the flavour of these burgers by using Wattie's Curry Creations Korma or Butter Chicken Curry Paste. These are readily available in 80-gram sachets in the supermarket. Alternatively use 2 tablespoons of your favourite curry powder and 2 tablespoons of tomato paste.

allyson's tip

Filo pastry needs to be light and crisp when baked. To achieve this, the pastry sheets need to be generously buttered and then well cooked in the oven.

did you know

41% of New Zealanders eat processed potatoes at home fortnightly or more.

500 grams new potatoes,
  scrubbed and thinly sliced

1 small onion, peeled and
  finely chopped

1 teaspoon Gourmet Garden
  Garlic

350-gram packet Wattie's
  Frozen Free-Flow
  Chopped Spinach,
  defrosted and well
  drained

½ cup chopped fresh parsley
  or 3–4 tablespoons dried
  parsley

4 eggs

½ cup cream

½ cup grated cheese (Edam,
  Gouda, Colby or Cheddar)

18 sheets filo pastry

100 grams butter, melted

200 grams feta, crumbled

spinach and potato filo pie

serves 6–8

preparation time **30 minutes** cooking time **45 minutes**

Cook the potatoes in boiling salted water for 5 minutes, then drain well.

Heat a dash of oil in a non-stick pan and cook the onion and garlic until tender. Add the spinach and cook a further 1–2 minutes. Set aside and when cool add the parsley.

Lightly beat together the eggs, cream and grated cheese.

Lightly grease a 20-cm x 26–28-cm oblong metal flan tin. Place 2 sheets of filo pastry in the bottom of the dish allowing any overlap to hang over the sides. Brush with melted butter then top with a further 2 sheets. Repeat the process using 10 sheets of filo in total in the base.

Layer the potatoes evenly over the pastry. Cover with the spinach mix and feta.

Carefully spoon the egg mixture over the top.

Butter the remaining 8 sheets of filo and layer on top. Roll any overlap back towards the top of the pie to enclose the filling. Brush with any remaining butter.

Bake at 190 °C for 40–45 minutes until the pastry is delightfully golden. If the pie begins to brown too quickly, cover with a sheet of baking paper and/or lower the pie in the oven.

allyson's tip

Gnocchi are tiny dumplings and they can be made from a pasta dough, potato or pumpkin, or semolina base. Look for them ready to cook in the chiller section of your supermarket. They keep well frozen and can be cooked straight from the freezer.

2–3 spring onions, trimmed
and finely chopped

150 grams mushrooms,
sliced

400-gram can Wattie's
Italian Style Tomatoes

½ cup red or white wine

1–2 tablespoons capers,
chopped

¼ cup green stuffed olives,
chopped or halved

¼ cup torn fresh basil leaves
or parsley

400 grams pre-made potato
gnocchi

¼–½ cup finely grated
Parmesan or Cheddar

potato gnocchi with herbed tomato sauce

serves 2
preparation time **10 minutes** cooking time **10 minutes**

Heat a dash of oil in a non-stick frying-pan and cook the spring onions and mushrooms for 2–3 minutes until tender. Add the tomatoes, wine, capers, olives and basil or parsley. Simmer uncovered for 5–6 minutes.

Cook the gnocchi for 3–4 minutes in a large pan of boiling salted water. Gnocchi is cooked when it rises to the top of the boiling water. Do not over-cook or it will be mushy. Drain well and arrange the gnocchi in 4 warmed serving bowls.

Spoon over equal amounts of the tomato sauce and scatter each with a little cheese. Place under a hot grill for about 2 minutes to brown the cheese.

3 tablespoons Gourmet
  Garden Basil

2 tablespoons toasted pine
  nuts, chopped

2 tablespoons finely grated
  Parmesan

2 tablespoons oil

2 teaspoons Gourmet
  Garden Garlic

4 Tegel fresh boneless
  chicken breasts

4–8 rashers rindless streaky
  bacon

700-gram bag Wattie's
  Rosemary and Garlic
  Potato Roasters

4 small tomatoes

1 red onion, peeled and cut
  into 8 wedges

4 courgettes, trimmed and
  halved lengthwise

bbq pesto chicken with roasters and vegetables

serves 4

preparation time **30 minutes** cooking time **30 minutes**

Mix together the basil with the toasted pine nuts, Parmesan and half the oil and garlic.

Cut a pocket into the side of each chicken breast. Divide the pesto into 4 equal amounts and use to fill each chicken breast pocket. Wrap one or two bacon rashers around each breast and secure with a toothpick.

Cook over a moderately hot barbecue for 25–30 minutes, turning regularly.

About 15 minutes before the chicken is cooked, toss the potato roasters onto a lightly oiled barbecue plate. Barbecue the potato roasters for about 15 minutes, turning occasionally.

Combine the remaining garlic and oil and brush over the prepared vegetables. Barbecue these beside the roasters for 5–7 minutes or until tender. Serve the chicken sliced, accompanied by the barbecue roasters and vegetables or salad.

allyson's tip

For those without a fan-
bake option, cook at 220 °C
for the same time.

116

500 grams lean beef mince

1 onion, peeled and finely chopped

1 carrot, halved and thinly sliced

2 stalks celery, trimmed and sliced

2 tablespoons Wattie's Tomato Paste

400-gram can Wattie's Tomatoes Chopped in Juice

½ cup stock or water

400-gram bag Wattie's Frozen Homestyle Mashed Potato

1 chorizo sausage, halved and sliced

¼ cup red wine

1 tablespoon chopped fresh thyme

café-style cottage pie

serves 4

preparation time **15 minutes** cooking time **45 minutes**

Quickly brown the mince in a dash of oil in a hot frying-pan, breaking up the mince with the back of a spoon as it browns. This is best done in two batches. Remove from the pan and set aside.

Add an extra dash of oil to the frying-pan and gently cook the onion, carrot and celery until crisp and tender, but not brown. Increase the heat and add the tomato paste and cook, stirring for one minute. Pour over the tomatoes and water and stir to combine. Return the browned mince to the sauce, cover and simmer gently for 15 minutes.

Place the mashed potato in a microwave-proof bowl, cover and microwave on high power (100%) for 8–10 minutes.

Spoon the mince into two small ramekins for the children, set aside. Add the chorizo, wine and thyme to the remaining sauce, spoon into two large ramekins for adults. Top with hot mashed potato.

Fan-bake at 200 °C for 10–12 minutes or until hot and golden (see allyson's tip).

Serve with your favourite green vegetables on the side.

1 onion, peeled and finely sliced

250 grams mushrooms, sliced

1 green capsicum, diced

1 carrot, peeled and grated

½ cup tomato paste

400-gram can Wattie's Pesto Style Tomatoes

¼ cup torn fresh basil l eaves or 2 tablespoons dried basil

2 tablespoons chopped fresh oregano or 2 teaspoons Gregg's Dried Oregano

750 grams starchy potatoes, peeled and thinly sliced

200 grams fresh lasagne sheets

350 grams frozen spinach, thawed and well-drained

400-gram can Wattie's Creamy Mushroom and Herb Pasta Sauce

vegetarian lasagne

serves 6

preparation time **40 minutes** cooking time **45 minutes**

Heat a good dash of oil in a non-stick pan and cook the onion, mushrooms, green capsicum and carrot for 3–4 minutes until the vegetables have wilted a little bit.

Increase the heat, add the tomato paste and cook a further 1–2 minutes. Add the tomatoes, basil and oregano and stir well. Set aside.

Cook the potatoes in a pot of boiling salted water for 5 minutes, drain well.

Spread half a cup of the tomato mixture into the base of a lasagne dish. Place a single lasagne sheet on top. Spread over half of the spinach and half of the remaining tomato mixture, half of the cooked potatoes and half of the pasta sauce. Top with a second layer of lasagne, followed

by the remaining spinach, tomato mixture, potatoes and pasta sauce.

Bake at 180 °C for 45 minutes until golden brown. Leave for 10 minutes before serving.

allyson's tip

This lasagne can easily be frozen and reheated at a later date. To do so, cool well, cover thoroughly to avoid freezer burn and freeze. Defrost during the day or overnight before reheating.

500 grams lean beef mince

1 onion, peeled and finely sliced

2–3 stalks celery, trimmed and sliced

535-gram can Wattie's Just Add Cottage Pie Simmer Sauce

½ cup water or beef stock

2 tablespoons chopped fresh thyme or parsley or 2 teaspoons dried thyme or parsley

600-gram bag Wattie's Frozen Kiwi Classics

6 tablespoons milk

home-style cottage pie

serves 4

preparation time **20 minutes** cooking time **25 minutes**

Brown the beef mince in a dash of oil in a deep non-stick frying-pan, breaking it up with the back of a spoon. This may be best done in two batches. Remove from the pan and set aside.

Add the onion and celery and pan-fry until tender, but not brown.

Pour in the simmer sauce and water or stock. Stir in the thyme or parsley and season. Return the browned mince to the sauce and simmer gently for 10 minutes.

Spoon the meat into a lasagne-style dish and level out with the back of a spoon.

Tip the frozen vegetables into a large microwave-proof bowl and cover loosely with plastic wrap. Microwave on high power for 8 minutes, stirring once during cooking. Mash well and stir in the milk. Season if wished. Spoon over the mince mixture.

Bake at 190 °C for 20–25 minutes or until hot and golden.

did you know

In the early days of the potato's introduction into Europe, the humble spud was viewed with much disdain. In France it was thought to cause leprosy. Some Protestant sects regarded it as ungodly as it was not mentioned in the Bible.

did you know

Classic International
Potato Dishes:
- Poland – Latkes (grated, fried pancakes)
- Belgium – Pommes frites (deep fried sticks)
- France – Lyonnaise (sautéed with onion and butter)

- Ireland – Colcannon (sautéed with onion and butter)
- Spain – Patatas bravas (cubed and fried in a garlic sauce)
- Greece – Skordalia (puréed with garlic and olive oil)
- England – Baked

(unskinned and oven baked)
- Italy – Gnocchi (small poached dumplings made with potato, flour and egg)

500 grams skinless chicken thigh fillets

1 red onion, peeled and thinly sliced

2–3 stalks celery, thinly sliced

410-gram can Wattie's Cream Style Corn with Bacon

½ cup sour cream or lite sour cream

¾ cup chicken stock or water

2 tablespoons chopped fresh thyme or 1 teaspoon dried thyme

500-gram bag Wattie's Frozen Golden Heart Potato Pom Poms

chicken and corn bake with pom poms

serves 4

preparation time **20 minutes** cooking time **35 minutes**

Cut each chicken thigh fillet into 6 pieces. Heat a non-stick frying-pan with a dash of oil and brown the chicken evenly. Scatter into an ovenproof dish.

Add the red onion and celery to the pan and cook for 3–4 minutes. Stir in the corn, sour cream, chicken stock or water, and thyme and heat through without boiling. Pour evenly over the chicken.

Arrange the pom poms on top.

Bake at 190 °C for 30–35 minutes or until piping hot and golden.

allyson's tip

Seasoned flour is prepared from standard white flour seasoned with salt and pepper and a pinch of mustard powder if you have it.

4 chicken leg and thigh portions, skin on

2 tablespoons seasoned flour (see allyson's tip)

about 6 sprigs fresh rosemary

1 lemon, quartered

1 onion, peeled and thickly sliced

2 rashers rindless bacon, diced

600-gram bag Wattie's Frozen Traditional Vegetable Roasters

quick roast chicken

serves 4

preparation time **15 minutes** cooking time **45 minutes**

Dust the chicken portions with a little seasoned flour. Place half the rosemary sprigs in the base of a roasting pan. Arrange the chicken portions, lemon and onion slices on top. Scatter over the diced bacon.

Arrange the vegetable roasters on a separate roasting tray and scatter with the remaining fresh rosemary sprigs.

Fan-bake the chicken at 190 °C for 15 minutes and then add the roasters to the oven and continue cooking for a further 30 minutes or until the chicken is tender and the roasters are golden and cooked.

Serve the roast chicken and vegetables with your favourite gravy or Wattie's Bit on the Side Sauce.

on the side

600 grams potatoes

2–3 tablespoons butter

¼ cup cream or whole milk

salt and ground white
    pepper to taste

classic potato mash

serves 4
preparation time **10 minutes** cooking time **15 minutes**

Cut the potatoes into even-sized pieces and cook in boiling salted water for around 12–15 minutes or until tender. Do not over-cook as the potatoes will fall to pieces and make a watery mash.

Drain and return the potatoes to the saucepan on a very low heat. Add the butter and cream or milk and mash. Beat the potatoes well with a wooden spoon until light and fluffy. Season to taste with salt and white pepper and serve immediately.

smashed potatoes
Follow the recipe as above, but wash the potatoes and do not peel. Mash coarsely.

allyson's tips

· Never be tempted to
mash potatoes in a food
processor. The resulting
mess will only be gluey or
claggy. This is due to the
blade which, with its harsh
action, breaks down the
starch molecules.

· It is possible to season
potatoes with black pepper,
however the black specks
can look like the flies have
walked over or through
the mash.

spring onion and cream
  cheese potato mash

600 grams starchy
  potatoes, peeled

½ cup cream cheese or lite
  cream cheese

3–4 spring onions, trimmed
  and finely chopped

milk for mashing

curry and cashew
  potato mash

600 grams starchy
  potatoes, peeled

2–3 tablespoons Malay
  curry paste (see page 66)

25 grams butter

milk for mashing

¼ cup toasted cashews

1 tablespoon crushed,
  toasted coriander seeds
  (optional)

1 tablespoon chopped
  fresh coriander

roasted garlic potato mash

600 grams starchy
  potatoes, peeled

1 bulb roasted garlic
  (see allyson's tips)

4 tablespoons quality olive
  oil or 4 tablespoons
  butter

milk for mashing

¼ cup chopped toasted
  walnuts

2 tablespoons fresh
  thyme leaves

mashed potatoes

**spring onion and cream cheese
potato mash**
serves 4
preparation time **10 minutes**
cooking time **15 minutes**
Cut the potatoes into even-sized
pieces and cook in boiling salted water
until tender. Drain.

Add the cream cheese and spring
onion and mash with a little extra milk
until smooth. Season if wished.

curry and cashew potato mash
serves 4
preparation time **15 minutes**
cooking time **15 minutes**
Cut the potatoes into even-sized
pieces and cook in boiling salted water
until tender. Drain.

Add the curry paste, butter and
sufficient milk to mash to a soft
consistency. Stir in the cashews,
coriander seeds (if using) and
coriander. Season if wished.

roasted garlic potato mash
serves 4
preparation time **5 minutes**
cooking time **15 minutes**
Cut the potatoes into even-sized
pieces and cook in boiling salted water
until tender. Drain.

Cut the garlic in half horizontally and
squeeze the pulp into the potatoes. Add
the oil or butter and mash with extra
milk until smooth. Season with salt and
pepper if wished. Stir in the walnuts and
fresh thyme leaves before serving.

allyson's tips

- To roast garlic – drizzle the garlic with a little oil and wrap the whole garlic bulb in foil. Bake at 180 °C for 1 hour or until soft in the centre when tested with a skewer. Cool.

- Making bread? Use cold water from boiling potatoes, yeast loves it and your loaf will have a lovely light texture.

mashed kumara with
   lemon and thyme
600 grams red-skinned
   kumara, peeled
50 grams butter
1 tablespoon fresh thyme
   leaves
1 lemon, grated rind
¼–½ cup hot milk

jamaican mashed kumara
600 grams orange-fleshed
   kumara, peeled
1 orange, grated rind
2 tablespoons dark rum
25 grams butter
¼ teaspoon ground
   cinnamon

mashed kumara

**mashed kumara with lemon
and thyme**
serves 4
preparation time **10 minutes**
cooking time **15 minutes**
Cut the kumara into even-sized
pieces. Cook in boiling salted water for
15 minutes or until tender. Drain well.

Mash thoroughly. Beat in the butter,
thyme, lemon rind and sufficient milk
to make a soft mash.

jamaican mashed kumara
serves 4
preparation time **10 minutes**
cooking time **15 minutes**
Cut the kumara into even-sized pieces
and cook in boiling salted water for 15
minutes or until tender. Drain well.

Mash until smooth. Beat in the orange
rind, rum, butter and cinnamon.

allyson's tip

Mashed kumara with lemon and thyme: The red-skinned kumara will require more milk for mashing than other varieties as they are much dryer. Have the milk hot, to avoid cooling off the mashed kumara.

allyson's tips

- If you are serving the roasted potatoes and kumara with a roast of meat, it is a good idea to use any fat that has collected around the meat as it cooked. It will impart a delicious flavour to the roast vegetables.

- If you roast potatoes beside a piece of meat, they will be less crisp, but have a wonderful flavour.

600 grams starchy
   potatoes, scrubbed
¼ cup oil or butter
salt and pepper

perfect roast potatoes

serves 4–6
preparation time **5 minutes** cooking time **40 minutes**

Peel the potatoes (if wished) and cut into equal-sized large pieces.

Par-boil in salted boiling water for 5 minutes, drain well and dry on absorbent paper.

Run a fork gently over the potatoes if wished to fluff up the outside.

Brush liberally with or toss in the oil or melted butter. Arrange on a baking paper-lined tray and sprinkle with salt.

Bake at 220 °C or fan-bake at 200 °C for 25–30 minutes (cooking time depends on the size of the potato portions) until golden and crisp on the outside and soft and tender on the inside. Serve hot.

allyson's tips

- The best kumara for roasting are the classic red-skinned Owairaka Red or Toka Toka Gold.

- Owairaka Red kumara will take longer to cook than other varieties.

- When peeling kumara, keep under water once peeled to stop discolouration.

- Like roasting potatoes, if you are able to coat the kumara in fat from a roast, they will be so much more delicious when served.

600 grams kumara, well
  scrubbed
¼ cup oil or melted butter
salt and pepper

perfect roast kumara

serves 4
preparation time **5 minutes** cooking time **35–40 minutes**

Peel the kumara if wished and cut into
long boat shapes.

Toss in the oil or melted butter and
season liberally. Arrange on a baking
tray, lined with baking paper if wished,
or around a roast of meat.

Bake at 200 °C or fan-bake at 190 °C
for 35 minutes, turning occasionally
until golden and tender. Cooking time
is dependent on the size of the pieces.
Serve hot.

3 large starchy potatoes

2 red-skinned kumara

2 yellow-fleshed or orange-
    fleshed kumara

2 onions, peeled

1 handful garlic cloves,
    crushed and peeled

2 generous branches
    rosemary, stripped of
    leaves

¼ cup olive oil

1 tablespoon Gregg's
    Paprika

mixed roast potatoes with garlic, paprika and rosemary

serves 8
preparation time **10 minutes** cooking time **45 minutes**

Wash the vegetables and peel if
you wish.

Cut the vegetables into chunky pieces
and place in a roasting dish. Cut the
onion into chunky wedges and add to
the roasting dish with the garlic,
rosemary, oil and paprika. Season
liberally with salt and pepper and
then toss.

Roast at 200 °C or fan-bake at
180 °C for 45 minutes or until
golden and crispy.

4 even, medium-sized
    starchy potatoes, peeled
2–3 tablespoons oil or
    melted butter
¼ cup freshly grated
    Parmesan

hasselback potatoes with parmesan

serves 4
preparation time **10 minutes** cooking time **40 minutes**

Cut a thin layer off the base of each potato so that they sit flat on a chopping board.

Using a sharp small knife make thin cuts cross-wise down the potatoes, without cutting all the way through.

Brush the potatoes with oil or butter and place on a baking paper-lined tray.

Bake at 190 °C for 20 minutes. Sprinkle each potato with an equal amount of the Parmesan and return to the oven for a further 15–20 minutes or until tender. Season before serving if wished.

index